An Elephant in the Room

An Equality and Diversity Training Manual

Blair McPherson

Russell House Publishing

Published in 2007 by:
Russell House Publishing Ltd.
4 St. George's House
Uplyme Road
Lyme Regis
Dorset DT7 3LS

Tel: 01297-443948
Fax: 01297-442722
e-mail: help@russellhouse.co.uk
www.russellhouse.co.uk

British Library Cataloguing-in-publication Data:
A catalogue record for this book is available from the British Library.

ISBN: 978-1-905541-16-4

Typeset by TW Typesetting, Plymouth, Devon

Printed by Cromwell Press, Trowbridge

Russell House Publishing

Russell House Publishing aims to publish innovative and valuable materials to help managers, practitioners, trainers, educators and students.

Our full catalogue covers: social policy, working with young people, helping children and families, care of older people, social care, combating social exclusion, revitalising communities and working with offenders.

Full details can be found at **www.russellhouse.co.uk** and we are pleased to send out information to you by post. Our contact details are on this page.

We are always keen to receive feedback on publications and new ideas for future projects.

Contents

About the Author

Blair McPherson is Director of Community Services for Lancashire County Council. He was previously Deputy Director of Social Services and before that Assistant Director of a large housing association. He originally trained as a teacher. Blair's passion for equality and diversity arose out of his first management post in inner city Birmingham. He has had a number of articles published in health, housing and social work journals addressing the issues faced by managers and human resource staff related to equality and diversity in the work place.

Acknowledgments

Brenda McPherson continues to be my biggest fan and my severest critic. This manual is all the better for our late night conversations.

A special thanks to Daphne.

How to Use this Manual

The materials in this manual have been designed to be used in small discussion groups.

They have been laid out so that they can be easily photocopied and issued as handouts to each member of the discussion group (this particularly applies to 'questions for group discussion' and 'further information').

Each section comprises:

- A short synopsis that the trainer can use as an introduction to the topic.

- A fuller description of the scenario.

- A series of questions that can be used to stimulate group discussion.

- References to further information so that individuals can explore the issues in more depth (these references are also good background reading for trainers).

This manual covers issues of race, gender, disability, faith, age and sexuality in relation to recruiting a truly representative workforce, getting the best out of a diverse staff group and delivering services to the whole community.

The material can be used equally well as part of an ongoing equality and diversity training programme or as a one-off staff meeting on the subject.

This approach to equality and diversity training has been found to be very effective in engaging staff at all levels because it allows people to relate to their own experience and to issues that they come across in their workplace.

Preface

This training manual is about equality and diversity in the workplace

The material itself and the discussion based approach aim to get people talking openly about race, gender, disability, faith, age and sexuality.

Most people are not racist, sexist, homophobic, ageist or prejudiced against faith groups and they don't deliberately make life harder for people with a disability. However, people are bombarded with negative stereotypes and myths in their daily lives. Their own limited opportunity for mixing with people different to them can lead to ignorance, insensitivity and unthinking prejudice. The material in this manual can be used to challenge these negative stereotypes, myths and prejudices by increasing awareness.

This manual gives managers, trainers and personnel staff the material to raise the profile of equality and diversity in their organisation. Taken as a whole the material in this manual will help:

- Change the way people think and behave at work.

- Help managers be better people managers.

- Help the organisation realise the full benefits of a diverse workforce.

- Increase the awareness and sensitivity of staff towards their colleagues and their customers.

- Create equality champions.

This manual deals with issues familiar to those working in health, housing and social services but will be equally relevant to staff in the private and voluntary sector.

Introduction

'An Elephant in the Room' is an expression to describe a big topic everyone is ignoring, pretending it doesn't exist because it is too scary or too difficult to deal with. Racism, sexism, ageism and homophobia – discrimination – can be a big, scary topic for some people.

The discussion articles, further information and good practice examples in this manual cover equality in the workplace and equality and diversity issues in service delivery.

The manual's starting point is that people need time and opportunity to think about and talk about equality and diversity issues. Managers need to establish a safe environment for this discussion to take place. The discussion articles and good practice examples encourage staff to identify the principles of good practice in equality and diversity; principles that apply whether talking about issues of race, gender, disability, faith, age or sexuality.

Simply talking about equality and diversity will not change the organisation's culture or people's behaviour. This requires everyone to recognise they have a responsibility for equality and diversity, not just managers, human resources and policy staff. Frontline staff need to acknowledge their responsibility for equality in their everyday dealings with service users and colleagues. For example, the way they respond to an enquiry, undertake an assessment, carry out a review or develop links with local community groups. The aim is to establish a culture where everyone takes responsibility for challenging racial and sexual stereotypes, ageist comments and insensitivity towards people with a disability. If we want people to take responsibility then we will need leadership from the top of the organisation, we will need managers to create a safe environment where people feel able to challenge. We will need champions to keep equality and diversity high on the organisation's agenda and we will need awareness training so that people are sensitive to the issues.

The material in this manual covers developing leadership from the top, creating a safe environment for people to challenge and be challenged, the role of equality and diversity champions and ways of raising awareness and sensitivity to equality and diversity issues.

Part One: Establishing Equality in the Workplace

Equality in the workplace is about ensuring people are not treated unfairly or discriminated against as a result of being different due to their race, gender, disability, sexuality, faith or age. This is not restricted to recruitment but extends to how people are treated at work. Do employees feel their manager and their organisation treat them fairly?

If all staff feel valued and respected, if they feel they are treated fairly, then the organisation they work for is unlikely to be characterised by bullying, harassment and discrimination. This requires managers to become more sensitive to people's needs and to improve their leadership skills by gaining insight into how their behaviour affects the people they manage.

'Equality and diversity' is therefore a management and a leadership issue – not something to be left to personnel and training staff.

Section 1 *Leadership and Equality and Diversity* identifies leadership as the missing ingredient when it comes to turning equality and diversity rhetoric into reality. This section also identifies ways of improving managers' people skills through coaching.

Equality in recruitment is covered in Section 2 *Head-hunters, Beauty Parades and Trial by Sherry* where the process for filling senior posts in local councils is critically examined as a way of prompting a discussion about fair recruitment processes.

In Section 3 *Supermarkets Show us the Way* the issues involved in recruiting staff who have a disability are identified. By using the example of people with a learning disability rather than a wheelchair user it is much more obvious that the barriers to recruitment are not physical but negative attitudes and inflexible recruitment policies. The discussion article shows how recruitment practices can be adjusted and how colleagues can be won over.

Most people would recognise it is unfair as well as illegal to turn someone down for a job or deny them a service because they are black, a woman or disabled. So how is it that there are so few black managers, senior women managers and disabled employees in health, housing and social care organisations? The answer is not overt discrimination but the result of stereotypes, myths, lack of awareness, ignorance and prejudice. To address this situation an organisation needs an equality and diversity training framework such as the one provided in Good Practice A *Developing an equality and diversity training framework for the whole organisation*. Such a framework will equip staff to manage a diverse workforce, deliver services to all sections of the community and promote best practice in relation to recruitment.

Part Two: Realising the Benefits of a Diverse Workforce

To realise the full benefits of a diverse workforce the organisation needs to identify the complex reasons why women, and people from black and minority ethnic groups, are under-represented in senior management posts. These patterns cannot be simply down to overt discrimination but require recognition that each individual experiences the world in a different way to you. This can affect their approach to seeking employment and promotion.

An organisation that values diversity, and employs people from a range of different backgrounds and experiences, recognises that it broadens and strengthens both the teams within it and the organisation as a whole. People who are different may bring something new to the team or organisation but only if their manager and the organisation values what they have to offer.

A well functioning and diverse workforce requires all staff to develop a sensitivity towards their colleagues by gaining knowledge and insight into how people who are different to you experience the world of work. This needs to be recognised as a two-way process in which the needs and perceptions of all people are identified.

Section 4 *Losing Balance on the Ladder* examines the reasons given by women and black staff for not applying for posts for which they have the qualifications and experience. It is clear that this has more to do with confidence than ability. In the case of black staff this is confidence in the recruitment process and for women it is a belief that they should feel confident they can do every aspect of the job before they apply. The implications of this for recruitment and staff development are examined. Good Practice B *Balanced interview panels* is an example of a measure taken to improve confidence in the recruitment process by the introduction of interview panels balanced in terms of gender and race.

If it is difficult to recruit black managers because the recruitment pool is so small then the alternative is to grow your own. Encouraging aspiring managers from under-represented groups is the aim of the training event described in Good Practice C *Climbing the ladder of success.*

An innovative approach to recruiting more black and minority ethnic staff is described in Good Practice D *How to recruit more black and ethnic minority staff.* This approach is based on establishing a database for those individuals who have expressed an interest in working in the organisation which is then used to deliver a direct mailshot of any relevant vacancies. In this way, details of people who applied but were unsuccessful are captured. Such individuals are often discouraged by their lack of success and think quite wrongly that there is no point in applying for further vacancies within the same organisation. This is a misunderstanding of how the recruitment process works but highlights the need to provide feedback to applicants, even those not invited to interview.

Having recruited staff from black and minority ethnic groups it is necessary to recognise that they may feel isolated as the only black person in the team or office and therefore need some additional peer group support. An example of such a black workers' support group is given in Good Practice E *Black workers development group.*

Part Three: Equality and Diversity as it Applies to Service Delivery

Equality and diversity is not restricted to employment, it also covers service delivery. Are people less likely to receive a service if they are black, gay, disabled, old, young or of a particular faith? Does the service offered take account of differences arising out of race, gender, disability, faith, age and sexuality or is everyone treated as if we all have the same needs, interests, circumstances and beliefs? Equality and diversity is not about treating everyone the same. The task is to help managers and staff understand this and explore what this means for their team, their service and their place of work.

Applying equality and diversity to service delivery is what managers say they struggle with most. Section 5 *Faith, Tolerance and the Acceptance of Diversity* recognises that managers often feel confused by the apparent contradictions when the Muslim community or the Gay community don't speak with one voice. The section examines the difference between faith and culture as a way of explaining the apparent contradictions and the implications for consulting about how best to provide services.

One of the most commonly expressed concerns is how can a white manager like me know what services to provide to people of a different race or faith. The same comment could of course be made about being an able-bodied heterosexual. The answer is the same – ask! In Section 6 *Chinese Lesson* the setting up of a culturally appropriate service and the issues it raised are discussed. Information and guidance on providing culturally appropriate care is given in Good Practice F *Culturally appropriate care.*

Specific guidance to managers is offered in Good Practice G *What can I do as a manager?*

To date, most of the attention around equality and diversity has focused on issues of race, gender and disability. Very little attention has been paid to issues of sexuality and its implications for providing health, housing and care services. Section 7 *Old and Gay* discusses Age Concern's research and its implications for meeting the health, housing and social care needs of older people who are gay, lesbian, bi-sexual or transsexual. It also provides an opportunity to examine the general issues of sexuality in service delivery. Good Practice H *Civil partnerships and sexuality* is an example of how to provide a sensitive and appropriate service in relation to arrangements for civil partnerships.

Part Four: Creating the Opportunities for Staff to Challenge and be Challenged

Getting people to talk openly about race, religion, gender, disability, ageism and sexuality involves creating a safe environment for people to say what they are really thinking and about creating appropriate opportunities for people to be challenged or supported. This will involve changing the way some people think and behave at work by identifying the questions people really want to ask but are reluctant to for fear of being labelled ageist, racist, sexist or homophobic. It means identifying stereotypes, myths and prejudices and challenging them.

Most people are not racist, sexist, ageist, homophobic or insensitive to people with disability, but they are bombarded with negative stereotypes and myths in their daily lives. If they have limited opportunities for mixing with people different to them this can reinforce ignorance, insensitivity and unthinking prejudice. Opportunities need to be created to challenge these negative stereotypes, myths and prejudices.

Section 8 *Creating a Safe Place* identifies what managers need to do if they want staff to discuss issues like race, faith and sexuality openly. This involves making it easier for people to raise issues of discrimination without fear of being labelled a troublemaker. It also involves having appropriate support arrangements for managers and not automatically labelling them bad managers if they are the subject of a harassment, bullying or racism claim.

Raising the profile of equality and diversity issues and encouraging people to talk openly involves finding innovative ways of encouraging staff to say what they are really thinking, to get the hot issues out into the open. This gives the organisation/senior managers the opportunity to challenge myths and explain policies.

Section 9 *Challenging Racism by Letting People Have Their Say* shows how an organisation used its intranet to get these questions out in the open – and answered – however uncomfortable the questions might be. A lot of the questions came from a two-day equality and diversity awareness course, fuller details of which are set out in Section 14 *An Equality and Diversity Training Course for Managers*. Some of the more controversial 'frequently asked questions', along with the answers, are to be found under Section 13 *Frequently Asked Questions.*

To promote good practice and keep equality and diversity high on the organisation's agenda requires equality champions. People at all levels within the organisation who are prepared to put time and energy to raising awareness around equality and diversity issues. In Section 10 *We are the champions* tackles the inertia and lack of passion that characterises most organisations and groups set up to address equality issues. Unlike nominated representatives, champions identify themselves, they don't represent a team or service area; what they have in common is a commitment to equality and diversity. The section explains what champions do on a day-to-day basis, how they were identified and how they are supported.

Throughout the manual, material has been introduced which provides an opportunity to challenge negative stereotypes, myths and ignorance. Ageism and homophobia are issues that are all too often neglected in health, housing and social care services. Ageism is widespread in society. It would be naïve to think it was not present in health, housing and social care services.

In Section 11 *I Hope I Die Before I Get Old*, a survey to identify managers' attitudes to old age is discussed. Some of the managers in the survey worked in specialist services for older people, others worked in a range of services. The aim of the survey was to raise awareness about ageism and encourage discussion amongst senior and middle managers. A simple and effective technique was used to get a quick and high response rate. A one-question questionnaire was sent by e-mail to 71 senior and middle managers working in a range of services. The e-mail required managers to select one of six responses. Sixty-four replies were received.

When it comes to sexuality does the number of gay characters in popular television programmes reflect a change in attitude towards gay people? Is this reflected in the workplace? In Section 12 *Gay May be Trendy But Have Attitudes Really Changed?* the outcome of a workplace survey is used to stimulate discussion and challenge stereotypes. In the survey staff are asked to respond to two workplace scenarios, one involving an invitation from a gay colleague to go for a drink after work and the other involving a male colleague who announces he intends to live as a woman. In the further reading suggestions the website for Stonewall is given. Stonewall offers advice and support to organisations in terms of training and awareness-raising around the issues of sexuality and advice on how to support gay employees.

The material in this training manual will allow groups of staff to explore equality and diversity issues and give staff a greater awareness and sensitivity about those who are different to themselves. It will assist an organisation to create a safe environment in which to challenge and be challenged, to develop equality and diversity champions and to reinforce the leadership role in equality and diversity.

Part One

Establishing Equality in the Workplace

Section 1
Leadership and Equality and Diversity

Leadership is the missing ingredient when it comes to turning equality and diversity rhetoric into reality. But how do you challenge the way managers behave and improve their people skills?

In Lancashire we have the same problems as everywhere else. How to get more women into senior management posts, how to get more people from ethnic minority groups into management posts, how to get more people with a disability into employment with us, how to increase the take-up of services by people from black and ethnic minority groups. We are adopting familiar strategies to tackle these problems. We monitor recruitment in terms of gender, race and disability. We set targets based on local population profiles. We provide staff and managers with awareness training and we give equality and diversity a high profile within the directorate. But something has been missing. The policies and strategies are right but progress has been disappointingly slow. We think the missing ingredient is leadership.

Leadership is not restricted to what managers at the top of the organisation do. Leadership when it comes to equality and diversity is about how all managers behave. If staff feel valued and respected, if they feel that they are treated fairly, then the organisation is unlikely to be one characterised by bullying, harassment and discrimination.

How managers treat their staff is crucial but in turn managers need to feel valued, respected and trusted by their managers. In this respect senior managers do need to lead by example but what counts is how your immediate manager behaves.

Another way of expressing this is that managers need to be good people managers. Managers are often appointed as a result of their professional expertise. People management skills have to be learned in the same way financial management skills have to be learned. However, people management skills are not learned in the same way.

The policies on recruitment and selection or absence management can be taught but it is the skill with which managers apply these policies that will determine whether staff feel valued, respected or treated fairly.

Improving managers' people skills requires an approach that develops the individual's insight into the impact their behaviour has on others. 360-degree feedback from colleagues is one way of managers finding out how their behaviour impacts on those they manage and those they work with. Myers-Briggs psychometric assessments will give the individual an understanding of their own preferences and therefore their strengths and potential blind spots. Building on this information requires the opportunity to receive some one-to-one coaching. The idea is for a specialist coach to observe the individual in action and give them detailed feedback. In this way the individual will be helped to develop greater insight into how their behaviour in a range of management settings impacts on others and how by making adjustments and trying different approaches they can be more effective leaders.

In Lancashire we have introduced executive coaching for senior managers and the next tier down (25 people). We are using two external management consultants to deliver the Executive Coaching Programme. A coach spends the equivalent of two days observing the individual in a range of activities including leading a team meeting, giving a supervision session, making a presentation to councillors or influencing a corporate working group. After each observation feedback is given and at the end of the programme individuals receive a detailed feedback report that is discussed with their coach. A copy of the report is also given to the line manager to be discussed and followed up in supervision.

Initially, senior managers were apprehensive. For many it was a long time since they had been given any impartial direct feedback about their behaviour. Most managers to date feel positive about the experience. In part this is due to the skill of the coach in making the experience feel positive; in part it is the fact that managers feel that this one-to-one work is of more relevance to them at this stage in their career than attending traditional management development training sessions.

Whether this investment in leadership development will change the way the directorate is viewed will be tested in the next staff survey, but if the results of the recent Investors in People accreditation are a reliable indicator then staff are already noticing a difference.

Things some staff said about their manager:

- That manager will never give a black person like me a job in their team.

- My manager has his favourites.

- The policies on annual leave and sickness absence are applied differently to different people.

- My manager doesn't like people going on courses because providing cover is difficult.

- My manager lets some people get away with murder but is always threatening me with disciplinary action.

- My manager doesn't believe in negotiating deadlines – she imposes them.

- We have noticed our female manager does not employ women with young children, and we think this is because she believes they will take time off to look after them.

- The boss takes all the school holidays off for annual leave but tells the rest of us to work out our annual leave arrangements between ourselves.

- Our manager makes decisions that affect all of us without consulting us. When we raised this she said 'That's what I am paid to do'.

- My manager doesn't challenge staff when they make inappropriate comments.

- My manager says their door is always open but if you try to raise something with him he says he is busy and can it wait until supervision.

- It is always the same managers on the recruitment panel. They have turned me down before so there is no point in me applying again.

- My manager just doesn't listen.

- My manager takes any questioning of their decisions as personal criticism.

- My manager makes it clear he doesn't want debate.

Section 1 **Leadership and Equality and Diversity**

Small group discussion questions

1. The quotes from staff clearly illustrate that some staff feel their managers don't act fairly. Is this evidence of discrimination, poor management or the fact that some staff will always complain if they don't get what they want?

2. How would you go about addressing the issues that staff raise in their comments about their managers?

3. What would an organisation look like that treated staff fairly and valued and respected staff?

4. How do you develop managers' people skills?

5. Executive coaching involves intensive one-to-one work. This is fine with a small group of 25 senior managers but how do you develop coaching and other management development opportunities for the large numbers of managers within the whole organisation?

Further Information
www.idea-knowledge.gov.uk – Improvement and Development Agency
www.eoc.org.uk – Equal Opportunities Commission

Section 2
Head-hunters, Beauty Parades and Trial by Sherry

Have you ever wondered how the top jobs in local councils are filled? What head-hunters do or what trial by sherry means? My personal experience is that the process of filling senior management posts is complex and drawn out over several days. Is this the best way to get the right person for the top jobs or an elaborate beauty parade?

Head-hunters, beauty parades and trial by sherry are the characteristics of modern senior management recruitment in local government. The standard process for recruiting staff in local government is fairly straightforward. The post is advertised in the professional press, candidates are selected for interview on the basis of their application form and the successful candidate is identified on the basis of their performance in the interview. The process is a lot more complex and drawn out when it comes to recruiting senior managers.

In most cases the recruitment process is contracted out to an executive recruitment agency. Their fee is based on their ability to deliver a strong shortlist from which the council can choose. The agency will ring people up and say 'Have you seen this post? Would you be interested in getting the details, if not do you know someone who might be?' This is called head-hunting. The first time you are head-hunted it is difficult not to feel flattered. However, you quickly come to realise that a lot of people are getting these calls and it does not indicate your name is being mentioned in high places for great things.

The first surprise is that head-hunters most often ask you to submit a CV rather than a local authority application form. From these CVs they draw up a long list of people to be invited to an 'informal interview'. This interview will be held in the up-market city centre offices of the recruitment agency – a world away from the average local authority office accommodation.

The informal interview is in fact a structured interview where you are asked the type of questions you would expect to be asked in a management interview. 'Tell us a bit more about your current post and responsibilities. How would you or your team describe your management style, what are your strengths and areas for development, what do you think are the key drivers for change in local government?'

Don't be surprised if the interviewers are two white males, the head-hunter with an HR background, the other 'a specialist adviser', someone who knows something about the area of work you have applied for. The specialist adviser is most often a current or recently retired senior local government officer or a director or chief executive. They will recommend to the leader of the council/cabinet members who should be short-listed and invited for what is most often a two-day assessment process.

Head-hunters are therefore influential people. They decide who to long-list and who to put forward for the short-list. Their activities fall outside the local authority's recruitment and selection process. Three big recruitment agencies have the largest share of the business so you are likely to keep coming across the same individuals if you are interested in a senior management post.

It has become the norm to have a two-day final assessment phase. This can involve psychometric tests, in-tray exercises, role play, an evening event and a bumpy trip around the patch in a draughty minibus. I quite enjoy the battery of tests and exercises; however, some people describe this as like sitting exams. Since everyone short-listed has a degree or equivalent and most have a management qualification I am not sure how these tests help select an applicant. Most candidates think that this part of the process is not going to determine who gets the job. However, candidates do think evening social events with elected members and partner agencies have the potential to rule you out of the running. These social events can be a formal sit-down meal at which the candidates change seats after each course so as to have the opportunity to talk to everyone or a buffet in which the challenge is to balance a plate of food and a drink whilst appearing intelligent. Such events are sometimes referred to as trial by sherry. The secret is not to eat or drink and to smile a lot.

Sometimes there is an opportunity to have a one-to-one with the chief executive or members of the senior management team. This is usually included to give you an opportunity to find out more about what it's like to work here. Never forget anything you say could be fed back to your disadvantage. Some people seem to delight in putting you off by telling you at this late stage how bad the budget position is or how poor the relationship is between officers and members. However, this could be just that they favour the internal candidate.

At some stage there will be a formal interview with the leader, cabinet members and opposition spokesperson and there will be the requirement to do a short presentation. This is where an interview panel of anything between 6–12 people makes the decision. A 10-minute presentation is followed by an interview that lasts no more than an hour. The presentation is a challenge; you are required to demonstrate clarity, brevity and passion. Content doesn't seem to be as important as you might expect because there isn't time to develop complex arguments and the audience is of mixed experience and knowledge.

The interview questions can range from the 'How would you solve our financial crisis?' to the politically sensitive 'What's your view on out-sourcing support services?' to an individual's pet subject 'Do you think officers should respond to councillors e-mails promptly?'

Successful candidates seem to be those who come over as confident and agreeable. Since all the candidates can demonstrate they have the experience, skills and knowledge to do the job, the senior management recruitment process is often described as a beauty parade. The final decision being based on whether you look and sound like the type of person the panel could work with.

Section 2 **Head-hunters, Beauty Parades and Trial by Sherry**

Small group discussion questions

1. Is the use of 'head-hunters' as described here compatible with equal opportunities? How could it be made more in tune with the spirit of equality of opportunity?

2. What groups could be disadvantaged by this approach to selecting senior managers? How?

3. What implications arise out of involving elected councillors – non executive board members – in the recruitment process and how could these be addressed?

4. Why should there be a different recruitment process for recruiting senior managers?

5. What would be the advantages and the disadvantages of giving head-hunters a brief to ensure the shortlist was balanced in terms of gender and race?

Further Information
www.idea-knowledge.gov.uk
www.SOLACE.org.uk
www.gatenbysanderson.com
www.pricewaterhousecoopers.co.uk
www.tribalresourcing.com

Section 3
Supermarkets Show us the Way

When people think of disability they tend to have a picture in their mind of a wheelchair user. But disability includes people with a learning disability. The barriers they face are not physical but negative attitudes and inflexible recruitment policies. *

The local supermarket puts most of us in social services to shame when it comes to employing people with a learning disability. We provide services like day care and supported housing to people with a learning disability but maybe because we see these people as clients rather than potential colleagues we don't offer them employment opportunities. The first barrier may be attitudes and prejudices. I once worked in a large social work office some distance from the local shops. On the same campus was a day centre for people with learning disabilities. An enterprising manager at the day centre had the idea of getting some of the day care attendees to make and sell sandwiches by taking them round the office workers. A varied selection of sandwiches was on offer but the venture failed because staff wouldn't buy sandwiches from people who looked like they had a learning disability. When pressed, one person cited 'hygiene' reasons.

The second barrier may be our difficulty in identifying what jobs people could do. This is more to do with our stereotypes and prejudices than a lack of job opportunities. We just can't imagine how someone with a learning disability would be able to do the type of jobs we have. Often this thinking applies to work experience placements where staff anticipate the individual will be a bit of a liability but it is only for half a day a week for a few weeks and it's a 'kind thing to do'. But often the experience challenges and changes these attitudes. Like our experience of Geoffrey (not his real name). The admin team have taken to Geoffrey in a big way, friendly, smiling, eager and helpful and he does all the boring jobs like photocopying, shredding, franking the post and filing. The other day he went round the office asking if anyone needed something doing because he had finished his work. No wonder he is popular. But moving from work experience to paid employment, a permanent job, presents another barrier.

---

* First published in *Community Care* 10/8/06 under the heading *A Job Well Done*.

The impact on a team of someone with a learning disability joining them should not be undervalued. A successful placement turns sceptical staff into advocates for employment opportunities for people with a learning disability and passionate supporters of their new colleague. They want placements to turn into permanent employment for the individual because they have seen that person grow in confidence. They have come to realise how important the job is to the individual, and the feelings of self-worth and value the individual gets from having a proper paid job for the first time in their lives. This comes as a shock to some staff long since used to the routines of work and the necessity of earning a living but then they think back to when they started work or when their son or daughter got their first job. They remember how proud they were as parents and then they realise how proud must be the parents of someone with a learning disability. Parents who never dared to have ambitions for their child. Staff come to realise how important the job is to the individual and how proud they are of their achievement. As one member of staff said to me 'Now I understand why it was so important to Geoffrey to have a staff ID badge'.

There is a view about that local government HR polices make it very difficult to recruit people with learning disabilities due to the requirement to fill vacancies through a competitive interview process. In the London Borough of Sutton they have used the 'reasonable adjustments' provision of the disability employment legislation to treat trial work placements as an alternative to the competitive interview in the recruitment process. However, it is not necessary to make special provisions for people with a learning disability or 'spare' them the experience of a competitive interview.

Recruitment and selection practices can be modified to make employment opportunities more accessible. Such an approach involves reviewing person specifications for basic grade posts to better match the skills required to do the job. For example, if we want some one to do photocopying, shredding and filing, then that is what we should recruit for rather than expecting the person to be multi-skilled in order to do multiple tasks. Such a post would be a Scale 1 admin as opposed to a Scale 1 to 3 admin.

Whilst the post would be open to anyone, the low grade, repetitive nature of the tasks and the limited responsibility would restrict who the post was attractive to. In addition, we know that most people with a learning disability looking for permanent employment are seeking part-time posts. Part-time work allows people to continue attending social centres and does not affect their benefits to such an extent as to make them worse off financially. These part-time posts can be as little as seven hours a week. Of course the aim must be to provide opportunities for full-time employment for individuals who want this.

Posts would be advertised in the job centres and local press as usual but would also be targeted at day centres and the employment service. Candidates would be short-listed and interviewed in line with the organisation's recruitment and selection policy. The interview questions would be set at a level appropriate to the post. In making an appointment, appropriate weight should be given to previous experience, evidence of good work attendance, punctuality, reliability and being conscientious. People with a learning disability could acquire this experience through work placements.

Our experience of work placements for people with a learning disability reflects the findings of national research, which shows that people with a learning disability have lower levels of absenteeism and are exceptionally reliable and conscientious. In general, once they have familiarised themselves with a task they need less supervision as they are less likely to get bored with routine tasks. Typically, managers describe employees who have a learning disability as 'wanting to learn', 'gets on with the job', 'popular with customers and staff', 'never late'. Don't assume from my example that people with a learning disability can't do complex tasks. MENCAP has produced a DVD endorsed by the CBI employers organisation which gives examples including a fork lift truck driver, a baker and someone who teaches others how to use computers.

Local authorities are large employers and should be leading by example. But all large employers should accept they have a social responsibility to their local communities and set recruitment targets for:

- Employing people with a learning disability.

- Identifying suitable posts.

- Revising person specifications.

- Creating opportunities for part-time working.

- Offering work placements.

Section 3   **Supermarkets Show us the Way**

Small group discussion questions

1. How would you go about persuading colleagues to offer a person with a learning disability a work placement in your team or office?

2. What support do you think you or your colleagues would need if you employed someone with a learning disability?

3. The team really take to a new colleague who has a learning disability but you notice other staff in the office are obviously 'uncomfortable' and ignore the individual. What do you do?

Further Information
WorkRight@mencap.org.uk

Good Practice A **Developing an equality and diversity training framework for the whole organisation**

This framework provides a structure within which directorates and direct service organisations can develop their training plans to meet the needs of their staff and the people they provide a service to.

Why do we need an equality and diversity training plan?

Most people would recognise it is unfair as well as illegal to turn someone down for a job or to deny them a service because they are black, a woman, or disabled. So how is it that there are so few black managers, senior women managers and disabled employees working for the County Council? The answer is not overt discrimination but can be the result of stereotypes, myths, lack of awareness, ignorance and prejudice.

Stereotyping – producing convenient mental pictures of what something is like, making assumptions based on prejudices rather than facts.

Prejudice – pre-judging or making up your mind about something based on either positive or negative feelings or ignorance of facts.

Discrimination – acting on these thoughts and feelings in a way that treats people unfairly or differently.

An equality and diversity training plan should give people the opportunity, time and space to examine stereotypes, explore myths, increase their awareness and become better informed in relation to race, religion, disability, gender, sexuality and age. Equality and diversity training should give managers and staff the confidence to be able to manage a diverse workforce and to deliver services to the whole community. It should help members, managers and staff find ways of dealing with the practical problems they face in providing services to a multi-cultural, multi-faith society. And promote and develop best practice in relation to recruitment and retention.

Who is equality and diversity training targeted at?

- Councillors/members of the board
- Managers
- All staff

Principles

Equality and Diversity training will:

- Cover recruitment, retention and service delivery.
- Cover all equality categories: race, faith, gender, disability, sexuality, those able to work full time, those working part time, temporary and permanent and those of all ages.
- Contribute to developing managers' people management skills to enable them to better manage a diverse workforce.

Key steps to producing an equality and diversity training plan

- Mapping to establish what equality and diversity training is currently available within directorates.
- Identify what equality and diversity training is required.
- Gap analysis.
- Examples of best practice.
- Recording and monitoring arrangements.
- Issues to be addressed (recruitment targets/service take-up/leavers).
- Checklist – questions the plan needs to answer.

Questions for directorates when developing an equality and diversity training framework

1. What categories should be covered by your equality and diversity training plan?
2. Should your plan cover recruitment, retention and service delivery?

3. Who is equality and diversity training targeted at?

   – training personnel

   – service delivery staff

4. Who is responsible for staff development with regards to equality and diversity?

5. Who is responsible for promoting best practice in recruitment, retention and service delivery?

6. Should staff development with regards to equality and diversity be limited to attendance on courses? What other learning opportunities should be made available?

7. Should training focus on legal responsibilities/duties, values and principles or case scenarios and issues related to the individual's work situation?

8. Should training focus on specific categories like race awareness or general equality and diversity awareness?

9. Should training focus on disability awareness or be specific to physical disability, learning disability or mental health?

10. Should training include:

    – service development

    – challenging stereotypes and myths

    – working with partners?

Part Two

Realising the Benefits of a Diverse Workforce

Section 4
Losing Balance on the Ladder

Why are women and people from ethnic minority groups under-represented in social care management and what can be done about it?*

I never think, 'Can I do that job?' I think, 'I fancy that job'. I'm never put off because the salary is too big. In planning my career I look to the job after next: 'What additional experience will I need to get from my next job to get me the big one?'

'I'm happy to consider a sideways move as part of the grand plan. I view secondments as the chance to raise my profile, extend my experience and acquire new skills. I'm prepared to take a risk with a secondment; after all, it is for a limited time only.'

'At some point I will need a formal management qualification, but if it is not part of the essential specification for a post I will not be put off simply because it is described as desirable. I do not feel the need to convince myself I can do the job; I just need to convince the selection panel. In any case, I will learn what I need to when I get the job. I understand the importance of knowing the management language and the latest "big new ideas". I'm prepared to go anywhere for that promotion.'

This approach may appear overconfident and overambitious, but it is not atypical of how men think about their careers. Although this is a caricature of a white male manager's attitude to career progression, it is different from the approach taken by women. This difference partly explains why women do not apply for management posts, particularly senior ones, in the numbers that would be expected, bearing in mind their representation in the social services workforce.

In our quest for a more balanced workforce, particularly at a senior level, we have been asking women why they have not applied for senior posts. They said they would only apply for a post once they were sure they would be able to do every aspect of the job. This contrasts with the typical male

---

* First published in *Community Care*, 4/1/06.

approach: 'I cannot do every aspect of the job, but I'll pick it up as I go along.' Women who had applied for posts often said that the deciding factor was being encouraged to do so by their line manager or someone else whose opinion they valued. Some women also reported being put off by a salary that was significantly higher than the one they already had, assuming that the salary reflected a much more demanding job with much higher expectations and an increased level of commitment in the form of longer hours. The male view would be that the salary reflected the market rate.

Recently we advertised several secondment opportunities. Not a single woman applied. When we pursued this, the reasons were that the post did not involve managing staff and that pursuing a secondment opportunity seemed to show a lack of commitment to the team. But the directorate views secondments as broadening an individual's experience and therefore a good career move. The assumption is that, after a secondment, the individual would be looking for a new job in which to use their newly acquired skills and experience.

Men and women seem to have a different approach to training and management qualifications. Women want to acquire skills to do the job better; men want to acquire qualifications to get a better-paid job.

Aspiring black managers have also reported feeling that they need to be able to show that they can do all aspects of a job before they apply. They have said that a significant factor in determining whether they will apply for a job is whether they are encouraged to do so by their line manager or another senior manager. From the comments of individuals it is clear that aspiring black managers have not tended to see secondment opportunities as the pathway to promotion.

Perhaps again this is because secondments often involve working in what are initially ill-defined areas where the individual has to cope with a higher level of ambiguity in the early stages, before gradually getting agreement on what the role involves and how it should be carried out. This being the case, it is difficult for the individuals to convince themselves that they have the skills and experience to do every aspect of the job.

Aspiring black managers often link career advancement with gaining formal qualifications. This may be because they feel they have already experienced discrimination when they were turned down for a post even though they had the same skills and experience as the successful candidate. Now, they see better qualifications as the only way to overcome such discrimination.

Feedback from black staff has indicated a lack of confidence in the recruitment process. It has been suggested that balanced interview panels in terms of gender and race and greater involvement by senior managers in management interviews would change perceptions. Changing recruitment processes and prioritising under-represented groups for management training would be a powerful message, but it would not address the gender and cultural differences identified from staff feedback.

If the need is to raise aspirations, increase confidence and encourage women and ethnic minority staff to apply for management posts, mentoring and coaching may be more effective.

Coaching and mentoring would need to be delivered in a working environment that valued diversity. It would be a mistake if we reinforced the view that to get on, women and black people need to adopt the behaviour of stereotypical white male managers. And it would not lead to better management.

The gender and cultural differences identified may not hold for a younger generation who have higher expectations, are more confident and are more career-oriented. The individuals that provided this feedback were from the directorate's equality and diversity champions group and the black workers support group, representing a cross-section of staff, both male and female, aspiring managers, middle managers and front-line staff. They are predominantly in the 35-plus age group. However, it is this sample of the workforce that forms the pool from which will be drawn the middle and senior managers of tomorrow.

What they said:

> *'Women do not achieve promotion as they lack male attributes.'*

> *'Having a mentor should not be seen as indicating that an individual is not doing their job well.'*

> *'I would guess that the female senior managers that we have are older, have children that are no longer at school or do not have any children.'*

> *'I have been told that I have only been successful because I am black.'*

> *'The reason why black staff want to be bolstered by qualifications when they go to interviews is that it gives them confidence to think that they can compete on a level playing field.'*

Section 4 **Losing Balance on the Ladder**

Small group discussion questions

1. Are we in danger of exaggerating gender and cultural differences?

2. The article suggests that cultural and gender differences are less apparent in the younger generation. Is this true or is it simply that they have yet to hit the glass ceiling?

3. Should under-represented groups be prioritised for coaching and mentoring opportunities or should all managers have these opportunities, and if so, how will this be resourced bearing in mind the numbers?

Further Information
www.womenandequalityunit.gov.uk – Women and Equality Unit
www.eoc.org.uk – Equal Opportunities Commission

Good Practice B **Balanced interview panels**

We have spoken to a lot of people from black and minority ethnic communities about their experience of applying for jobs. In response people have said that coming into a room to be faced by an all-white interview panel can be a little off putting and make them feel less comfortable. They suggested a balanced interview panel would make them feel less anxious and therefore more likely to come over better in the interview.

No one these days would think it acceptable or appropriate to have an all male interview panel.

The National Probation Service – Lancashire have appointed a number of diversity advisors to act in an advisory capacity to ensure that the application of policies is carried out fairly and is free from bias. There is particular emphasis on the recruitment and selection of staff. The job description used to recruit to these posts follows.

JOB DESCRIPTION

Employer: Lancashire Probation Board

Location of job: Various

Job title: Diversity Advisor

Job grade: Hourly paid (£14 per hour)

Responsible to: HR & Training Manager

Hours: As required

Other: Available at short notice on occasions

Overall purpose of job: To act as an external advisor to the National Probation Service – Lancashire to ensure that the application of policies is carried out fairly and is free from bias. Particular emphasis and involvement will be with Recruitment and Selection of staff.

Main activities/tasks:

1. To participate in the recruitment and selection of staff by:

    – Ensuring that candidates are treated fairly and equally in accordance with anti-discriminatory practices and current legislation.

    – Short-listing candidates against agreed criteria.

    – Attending interviews and scoring the performance of candidates against agreed criteria.

    – Undertaking the role of assessor at assessment centres.

    – Providing external advice and validation of the fairness of the selection process – by completion of a feedback sheet for the human resources team.

    – Advising the interview panel on potential areas of discrimination.

2. To provide advice or assistance in carrying out investigations for disciplinary, grievance and bullying and harassment matters.

3. To attend training for the role – e.g. R&S training, assessment centre briefings, investigations training.

4. To attend quarterly meetings to discuss diversity issues and to suggest areas for improvement.

Good Practice C **Climbing the ladder of success**

An organisation will find it difficult to help women and black staff into senior management posts if they are under-represented at first and middle management level. In some cases the issue is not about helping managers develop their careers but about helping people who aspire to be a manager get on the first rung of the management ladder.

This is a good practice example from Lancashire County Council of a one-day training event aimed at aspiring managers. Participants select from a range of one hour workshops.

Topics covered:

- How to sell yourself at interview.

- How to improve your presentation skills.

- How to prioritise your work.

- Understanding performance management.

- The manager's role in promoting quality.

- How to be an effective communicator.

- What you need to know about equality and diversity.

These events were targeted at women and black staff as under-represented in management posts. The events were run four times a year and workshops were adjusted in line with popularity and topicality. They were very popular because of the pick-and-mix style and the amount on offer in short bursts.

Good Practice D   **How to recruit more black and ethnic minority staff**

Lancashire Social Services worked with the management consultancy firm TMP to seek to increase the number of black and ethnic minority staff in line with population profiles.

Although this project was undertaken to improve recruitment of people from black and minority ethnic groups the findings have implications for recruitment from all sections of the community.

What did we do?

- Telephone interviews and focus groups with people who had applied for posts within Social Services but who had been unsuccessful.

- Focus group with new starters in Social Services.

- Focus group with HR staff in Social Services Directorate.

- Two focus groups with members of the public.

- All above with emphasis on people from black and minority ethnic groups.

- Focused on recruitment process for posts that required no previous experience or qualifications.

Main findings

- People think the County Council is a good employer.

- People don't know what job opportunities there are in the County Council.

- People didn't realise the County Council offered staff training and opportunity to gain professional qualifications.

What's different about this recruitment initiative?

The setting up of a database of people who have expressed an interest in working in the Directorate, which is then used to deliver a direct mailshot of any relevant vacancies.

Good Practice E   **Black Workers Development Group**

What is the Black Workers Development Group?

- The Black Workers Development Group (BWDG) is a forum for black* staff who work in Social Services in Lancashire.

- The group was formed by black staff in 2002.

- The BWDG is supported by the senior management team and is part of Lancashire County Council's equality and diversity agenda.

What is the aim of the BWDG?

- The BWDG is aimed at promoting the welfare, personal and professional development of all black workers within the Lancashire County Council – Social Services Directorate, through networking and sharing of experiences to maximise the potential of black workers in the workforce.

How often does the BWDG meet?

- Every two months at different venues around Lancashire.

- Line managers should support and encourage black staff to attend.

Who can attend the BWDG meetings?

- The BWDG meetings are open to all black staff working at all levels in Social Services.

What does the BWDG do?

- Provides a forum for black workers to meet.

- Provides a consultation forum for Social Services and Lancashire County Council.

- Promotes awareness of personal learning needs.

- Provides opportunities for personal and professional growth.

- Act as an agent for change.

- Promotes good race equality policies and practices.

---

* The term 'black' on this page refers to members of minority ethnic groups who are distinguished by their skin colour or physical appearance, and who may therefore feel some solidarity with one another by reason of past or current experience, but who may have different cultural traditions and values.

- Provides a forum for networking with other black workers support groups and agencies.

- Provides individual support.

- Challenges racism at an individual, cultural and institutional level.

- Promotes race equality at various forums through black worker representation.

Part Three

Equality and Diversity as it Applies to Service Delivery

Section 5
Faith, Tolerance and the Acceptance of Diversity

Examining the difference between faith and culture helps us better understand how to respond to the needs of a diverse workforce and diverse communities.

Tolerance of diversity

Differences mark people out, the colour of their skin, the clothes they wear, the language they speak, their religion, the way they speak and the way they look. The diversity of the human race can make us feel uncomfortable when we come into contact with people who are different to ourselves. I have heard people say they are uncomfortable in some formal events because they think other people are 'posh'. On a more serious note I have heard and seen how uncomfortable some people get in the presence of a member of staff who has a learning disability. Some people in a recent management survey said they would feel uncomfortable going into a gay bar. I have heard older people say that groups of young people outside the off-licence make them feel uncomfortable.

Feeling uncomfortable may be a natural reaction to being put in an unfamiliar situation or coming into contact with people who are clearly different to you. What is important is how we react to such situations; with suspicion and fear, withdrawing from such situations and avoiding them in the future, or with a willingness to overcome the initial anxiety, to keep an open mind, and to get to know people as individuals.

The difference between faith and culture

In my experience many staff struggle to understand why Muslim communities within Lancashire appear to have different views on what is and what is not acceptable behaviour. Staff are confused because in one locality the Muslim community may say men and women can't eat together for religious reasons and in another part of Lancashire the Muslim community may say it is perfectly acceptable for men and women attending a day centre to eat together in the same room. This apparent contradiction can be explained by reference to different cultures within the same religion. The culture is the local tradition, the way people have always done things; it is strongly influenced by family, friends and neighbours. Traditions are often challenged by the young and do change but the pace and extent of change differs from one community to another – hence different views by people of the same religion on what is acceptable.

It is not religion or faith that determines whether a Muslim woman wears the head to toe covering burqa – it's culture. That is, whatever is considered the norm or expected behaviour within the community where the individual lives. How else would you explain different practice between Muslim countries and between Muslim communities? In developing day services for Asian elders I am aware of communities where they find it perfectly acceptable for Muslims and Hindus to attend the same centre whereas a few miles away it is not, and Muslim men and women must have totally separate facilities so that they do not mix.

If you are providing services to a diverse population you should not make assumptions on the basis of religion or faith. You do need to be sensitive to cultural differences. What this means is taking the time to consult with people in the local community and asking people how they want their needs met. Community engagement at a neighbourhood level involving local people in how local services are delivered and developed is considered good practice irrespective of the ethnic or religious make-up of the local population.

Any consultation exercise will throw up a range of views so why is it we get confused and frustrated when the Asian community or the Muslim community don't speak with one voice? We would recognise that the Irish community in any of our big cities would be made up of people from Southern Ireland and Northern Ireland, people from rural communities and urban communities, Protestants and Catholics, people from professional backgrounds and manual workers, those who grew up in Ireland and those born in this country and those like me with nothing Irish about them except my name. We would not expect everyone to identify the same needs or be unanimous in how these needs should be met.

Tempting as it may be to put our trust in a few community leaders or the views of a representative from the Mosque or temple, it is unrealistic to think that these individuals will represent anything other than a section of the community. If we were consulting in your neighbourhood about a proposed housing development would you be happy for the local vicar, the youth centre worker and the chair of the Women's Institute to speak on your behalf?

What this means is that we have to work hard at getting to know local communities, particularly those different to our own.

Section 5 **Faith, Tolerance and the Acceptance of Diversity**

Small group discussion questions

1. For most of us, being made to feel uncomfortable happens only occasionally, but what about those people for whom it is a daily occurrence? What's it like to be the only woman in a large group of senior managers who insist on talking about football? What is it like to be the only wheelchair user in the building or the only black person in the team?

2. Identify examples of the difference between faith/religion and culture. What are the implications for service delivery?

3. How would you set about getting to know the local black and ethnic minority community? In consulting with this community what issues would you need to be aware of?

4. What lessons can be learnt from the debates about religion, culture and how some people dress?

Further Information
The importance of veils to the Muslim community http://news.bbc.co.uk/1/hi/world/middle_east/5411320.stm
Life behind the veil http://www.guardian.co.uk/religion/Story/0,,1889871,00.html
Headscarves are proving controversial in a number of countries http://news.bbc.co.uk/1/hi/world/europe/3476163.stm
Headscarves contentious clothes http://news.bbc.co.uk/1/hi/world/europe/3135600.stm
Integration http://www.guardian.co.uk/commentisfree/story/0,,1870962,00.html

Section 6
Chinese Lesson

How can white managers know what services black and ethnic minority people want?

In Birmingham a small group of us set about developing culturally sensitive services for Chinese people by listening to them.

We identified five different voluntary groups within the Chinese community to hear what they had to say. The Chinese community is made up of people from Hong Kong, the Chinese mainland and those from Taiwan. It includes Buddhists, Christians and Ancestor Worshippers; Cantonese, Hakka and Mandarin speakers; and people from rural and urban backgrounds. We were careful not to let the views of any one sector of the Chinese community dominate.

Chinese elders and their carers told us they wanted day care, respite care, home-care services and long-term residential care that is culturally sensitive and appropriate.

We needed to get the confidence of the Chinese community to convince them that we are able to plan a culturally sensitive service and that our staff were committed to this. We started to plan a day centre for Chinese elderly people by holding regular planning meetings with representatives from the Chinese community. We sought out a Chinese social work student to help us set up the day centre, and a social worker to supervise the student and work with the manager responsible for the day centre. This was to be a 20-place day centre, one day a week. We were advised that Tuesday was a day on which restaurants were closed and therefore the best day to offer day care.

When the opening day came it was a big occasion. Publicity attracted over 100 people, and the selling of the centre was *too* effective. The next Tuesday 50 Chinese elders turned up. Places were offered following a needs-based social work assessment and transport was provided, but we now operate a luncheon club and a drop-in centre for anyone who can make their own way. We had to fit into the needs of the Chinese community, not the other way round.

Chinese videos are shown and elderly people play mah-jong. There are posters of Chinese festivals on the walls. Chinese crockery is used and round tables have replaced the square dining tables so there is no head of the table. Some members of staff are Chinese and speak Cantonese. Traditional Chinese food is served. Lots of Chinese volunteers and relatives attend with their families and friends.

The day centre was housed in an existing centre open seven days a week. We simply earmarked Tuesday for Chinese elders. From that point on, only Chinese elders were offered day care on Tuesday. Existing day care attendees were offered the choice of continuing to come on Tuesday or be offered another day in the week. Some chose another day. Some were happy to continue on Tuesdays. At first we had day-care staff but no Chinese staff and no vacancies. We 'borrowed' a vacancy from another home with the agreement of a very supportive officer-in-charge. We were up and running with a re-allocation of resources.

Word of mouth in the Chinese community was seen as the best way to recruit, rather than an advert in the Chinese national paper. Interviews were conducted with the help of a Cantonese speaker from a voluntary organisation. Initially Chinese food was prepared by a volunteer who ran a takeaway and whose elderly relative was one of the first attendees. We were later successful in obtaining inner city partnership funding which enabled us to recruit a part-time Chinese cook and Cantonese speaking care assistant.

Day care has led to a take-up of other services by the elders, including respite care and in one case long-term care. We learnt of one elderly man in a psychiatric ward, isolated by language and cultural barriers and physically frail. The ward staff did not know what to do with him. He needed nursing care and so was admitted to a nearby nursing home to enable him to attend the day centre, have access to Cantonese speaking staff and be provided with Chinese food.

When we began this project we had no idea of the size of need within the Chinese community. But we did know that there was not a single Chinese person in any of the city's social services department's day centres.

In the first six months we received over 100 referrals. Most did not require day care but needed welfare and benefit advice, help with housing problems and access to health care. A social work assessment takes place on all referrals of clients with the help of a Chinese member of the centre's staff who acts as an interpreter.

We have the responsibility as managers to develop culturally sensitive services and to provide services in line with the local population profile. We have the power to do this, as illustrated by this example. As managers we will be judged by our effectiveness. Good intentions are not enough.

Section 6 **Chinese Lesson**

Small group discussion questions

1. In this example what does a culturally sensitive service look like?

2. In this example the criteria for eligibility for a service and even the definition of day care were changed in order to provide an appropriate service. What would be the implications of this approach for other services and other service users?

3. What sort of resistance could you anticipate from staff, service users and councillors if you proposed dedicating a centre or a service for the use of a specific ethnic minority group? How would you overcome this resistance?

4. Operating a service with staff who speak a service user's first language sends out a clear message to the community. What implications does this have for recruitment and pay and how would you address these issues?

Further Information
www.cre.gov.uk – Commission for Race Equality

Good Practice F **Culturally appropriate care**

Lancashire Social Services produced a commissioning strategy for minority ethnic groups entitled 'Culturally Appropriate Care'. The document was an adaptation of the booklet 'Culturally Competent Care' produced by Kent Social Services.

Introduction to 'Culturally Appropriate Care'

The Social Services Directorate has a strong commitment to racial equality, which is reflected in the Racial Equality Action Plan. This states how the Directorate will address the issues of low take-up of services, lack of knowledge about services, and perceptions within minority ethnic communities that insufficient account is taken of race, culture and religion in assessing need. As part of the Racial Equality Action Plan the Commissioning Strategy aims to 'mainstream' services to minority ethnic groups and promote community cohesion.

Mainstreaming services means moving away from a reliance on voluntary organisations supported by ad hoc grants, to providing services either in-house or by competitive tendering and formal contracts with the private and voluntary sector.

Where appropriate, this will involve commissioning from in-house providers, for example day care for Asian elders. In other instances this will involve commissioning from the independent sector, for example domiciliary support or rehabilitation schemes. In children's and family services this means recruiting more foster carers and adopters from minority ethnic groups, rather than relying on independent fostering agencies.

This means ensuring that family support services and services for children with a disability are culturally sensitive and appropriate, and where parents' first language is not English, bilingual workers or interpreters are available. This also takes account of, and being sensitive to, culture and religion in respect of what is considered appropriate and acceptable behaviour for young women within the community, which may mean providing single sex services. In all cases we will expect providers to be working in partnership with the local minority ethnic community.

The strategy recognises that Lancashire is a large and diverse county made up of 12 districts, ranging from inner city areas with all the associated problems, to rural areas with affluence and poverty often sitting side by side. Lancashire is a multicultural county with a sizeable Asian community. The minority ethnic communities are concentrated in certain neighbourhoods in Preston, Pendle, Burnley and Hyndburn.

The Directorate has agreed district commissioning plans for people with a learning disability, older people, people with mental health problems and people with a physical disability or sensory impairment. These plans have recognised that whilst the needs of people from minority ethnic communities may be the same as the rest of the community, meeting their needs will require service specifications which take account of culture and religion.

Whilst recognising the need to ensure that the social care needs of people from minority ethnic groups are appropriately met wherever they live in the county, the Directorate aims to focus efforts in certain neighbourhoods where the minority ethnic population is concentrated.

Further Information
http://www.lancashire.gov.uk/social-services/publications/commissioning-plans/culture-awareness.pdf
http://www.elsc.org.uk/knowledge_floor/database/html_extended_abstracts/0079584.htm

Good Practice G **What can I do as a manager?**

As a manager you have responsibility for recruitment, service delivery and the management and development of your staff.

Recruitment

- Balanced interview panels (see *Good Practice B*).

- Use person specifications that are inclusive rather than providing reasons to exclude people (even if this results in a large shortlist and having to interview over two days rather than one).

- Ask interview questions that establish the candidate's understanding of and commitment to equality and diversity.

Service delivery

- Ensure the ethnic origin and religion of all your service users is recorded.

- Visit mosques, temples and black and minority ethnic voluntary groups in your locality with a view to fostering better understanding and future collaborations.

- Make reception areas and meeting rooms reflect the ethnic diversity within your locality.

- Tap into the knowledge of black and minority ethnic staff.

- Speak at the local consultation forums within black and minority ethnic communities and listen to what people at these meetings are saying.

Manage and develop staff

- Support staff attending the black workers support group.

- Challenge racial stereotypes, myths and ignorance.

- Support staff who challenge racial stereotypes, myths and ignorance – don't allow them to be labelled difficult.

- Use material on the equality and diversity website, particularly the frequently asked questions to promote discussion in your team and with partner agencies.

- Ensure your staff know what the Race Equality Schem
  it.

- Increase the opportunities for contact between your s
  of the black and ethnic minority community through v
  placements.

- Actively promote the directorate's approach to equality

- Identify a champion within your team and encourage th
  Directorates Champion Group.

Section 7
Old and Gay

To date, most of the attention around equality and diversity has focused on issues of race, gender and disability. Very little has been done on sexuality and its implications for providing care services. This reflects a nervousness and uncertainty about how to explore issues of sexuality. Age Concern's recent work on sexuality in older people has offered the opportunity of raising awareness about how best to meet the social care needs of older gays, lesbians, bisexuals and transsexuals. It's also an opportunity to raise awareness about issues of sexuality in social care in general, whether they be around recruitment or service delivery.

Sexuality in old age seems to be a less threatening area to start exploring issues of sexuality for most staff, probably because older people are not considered to be sexual.

Older lesbians and gay men have been invisible within health and social care services because unlike other oppressed groups they can hide their difference and pass as heterosexual. In less tolerant times being openly gay would have resulted in discrimination. Prejudice, myths and stereotypes about gay people still exist. These beliefs are reflected in commonly held views about lesbian and gay men's suitability to look after children.

Myths and stereotypes

- Gay men are a sexual threat to children.

- Children growing up in lesbian or gay households will have a distorted view about what it is to be a woman or man.

- Lesbian and gay parents will transmit their sexuality to their children.

- Children will be stigmatised if they live in a lesbian or gay household.

Just as in the past health and social care professionals adopted a colour-blind approach to race, some professionals now consider lesbian and gay clients to be no different from anyone else.

A research report by Age Concern called *Opening Doors* (July, 2001) identified that older lesbians and gay men had unmet health and social care needs. The report provided advice to organisations on how to make their services more inclusive to this particular group. It covered awareness, sensitivity and the attitudes of those who work with and for older lesbians and gay men.

Through interviews with older lesbians and gay men they identified how the needs of these individuals may differ from the wider group. The experience of these individuals confirmed research that older lesbians and gay men are more likely to come to the attention of social care services as they do not have the same network of family support, having never married, and therefore having no children or grandchildren to support them in later life. Whilst other residents may be reminiscing about their life with their partners, older lesbians and gay men may be reluctant to join in as this may involve revealing a partner of the same sex. The care needs of an individual extend beyond their physical care needs to those of their emotional and sexual needs. If an individual has to deny who they are and what they feel, and is constantly aware of the disapproval of others, they are not having their care needs appropriately met. How would a residential home or a sheltered housing complex respond to an admission or application from a married couple? Would the response be different if the couple were of the same sex? What about a relationship that developed over time and the individuals concerned requested to share a bedroom or flat? What would the response be of staff? What would the response be of other residents or tenants?

The Age Concern report highlights the prejudice amongst residents that older lesbians and gay men are only too aware of, and suggests that it is the organisation's responsibility to challenge inappropriate and discriminatory attitudes amongst other service users.

Not surprisingly, the report also identifies that prejudice in the wider society is likely to rub off on care staff and that there is a need for specific staff training.

Legal, moral and business case for addressing issues of sexuality

Legal

The law has changed, with 'civil partnership' giving same-sex couples legal recognition and similar treatment to married people for tax, pension and tenancy rights.

Moral

It is the right thing to do. As an organisation we are committed to treating people with dignity and respect. This applies in the same way to their sexuality as it does to their race or religion. A positive attitude to lesbian or gay older people also offers reassurance to colleagues who may be anxious about being open about their sexual orientation in the workplace.

Business

The 'pink pound' reflects a recognition in the business world that the gay community is a significant market. This will apply to choices made for housing and care. 20 per cent of older lesbians, gay men and bisexuals indicate that they have no one to call on in a time of difficulty – a rate up to ten times higher than that seen in the general older population.

In response to the challenge of providing appropriate and sensitive care services to older lesbians and gay men, agencies like Age Concern Camden and Stockport have developed, and are delivering, dedicated projects.

Research into sexuality and older people has identified that their health and social care needs are at risk of not being appropriately met. This may be because people are reluctant to identify themselves as lesbian or gay, or because agencies and staff adopt a 'we treat everybody with the same attitude'. It may also be because of ignorance or prejudice on the part of staff.

The way to address this situation is to challenge myths and stereotypes, develop awareness and sensitivity in much the same way as we do in relation to issues of race, gender and disability. Such an approach to sexuality in old age clearly has implications for addressing issues of sexuality in general.

Section 7   **Old and Gay**

Small group discussion questions

1. What lessons from work around meeting the needs of ethnic minorities could be applied to meeting the needs of lesbian, gay, bisexual and transgender individuals?

2. What would a service look like that was welcoming to lesbians and gay men?

3. What are the advantages and disadvantages of developing services specifically for lesbians and gay men?

4. The article refers to lesbians and gay men, but are the issues the same for bisexual and transgender individuals?

5. One definition of a safe organisation is one in which people feel able to come out. How we treat lesbian and gay staff will be a good indication for people thinking about using our services. How should we go about making the organisation one in which staff feel comfortable about discussing their sexuality?

Further Information

www.ageconcern.org.uk

    Opening Doors 2001 a report by Age Concern

    'The Whole of Me' (2006 resource pack) Age Concern

www.stonewall.org.uk – Stonewall

www.cipd.co.uk – Chartered Institute for Personnel Development

Older Lesbians, Gay Men, Bisexuals and Transgender People (OLGBT) Housing and Care. *The Journal of the Institute of Ageing and Health*, October 2003.

Good Practice H   **Civil partnerships and sexuality**

An example of making a service appropriate and sensitive

The Civil Partnership Act 2004 allowed same sex partners to register their partnership (referred to wrongly in the press as 'gay marriages'). The local authority Registrars Service is responsible for recording births, deaths and marriages. Civil partnerships carried out by the local authority presented an opportunity to attract new business and new income but only if staff could be won over.

Initially, there was resistance from staff, ranging from 'It's not in my job description' to prejudice in the form of 'I don't agree with this type of thing'. The challenge was how to win the hearts and minds of staff and how to set up a new service that was appropriate and sensitive to the needs of gay men and lesbian women.

It was decided to go ahead and introduce this new service, despite the resistance of some staff, working in the first place with those staff who were keen and supportive. These staff later became champions. We didn't know what would make a good service so we asked gay people, as the experts, about their needs and wants. A small group was set up to help design some literature explaining how to go about booking a civil partnership and what the service offered. It was important right at the start to use the correct phraseology so that potential customers would know that the people involved in designing the service were themselves gay men and lesbian women.

Winning the hearts and minds of the staff involved awareness raising and training delivered by gay men and lesbian women. This was the first time some staff had the opportunity to meet and talk to openly gay people. The sessions were provided to managers and staff. The trainers explained why gay people might want to enter into a civil partnership, pointing out the reasons were the same as people who wish to get married e.g. make a legal bond, enter into a formal commitment and make a public declaration of their love.

The working group produced a leaflet 'How to Plan Your Civil Partnership'. They advised on marketing material and helped develop and test the ceremony. We established through extensive consultation with gay and lesbian groups that people did want a ceremony so we made it possible to offer the same things that we do for weddings: declaratory words, readings, music and even confetti.

Was it a success? – Yes, 514 same-sex people have given notice of intention of forming a partnership and 147 partnership ceremonies have been conducted so far (June 2006).

Part Four

Creating the Opportunities for Staff to Challenge and be Challenged

Section 8
Creating a Safe Place

To tackle racism and other forms of discrimination you need to create safe places for staff to talk about these issues openly.

Institutional racism – that is attitudes and behaviour which amount to discrimination through unwitting prejudice, ignorance, thoughtlessness and racist stereotyping – exists and persists in organisations. It persists despite policies, training, awareness raising, recruitment strategies and monitoring arrangements because most organisations are not safe enough places to discuss these issues openly. This is also true of other forms of discrimination.

In an organisation that's not safe enough staff don't feel able to raise issues of discrimination for fear of being labelled a trouble-maker or playing the race card. That is where someone claims to have been treated unfairly then states the reason for this is because they are black.

A very small number of people will see conspiracies against themselves and evidence of discrimination everywhere. They will be quick to use formal procedures and they will pursue these procedures through an appeal system until they have exhausted every avenue. Such individuals take up a disproportionate amount of management time and energy. When the individual in question is black, managers don't feel able to say that these individuals are exploiting the system for fear of being called racist.

Senior managers don't want to delve too deeply for fear of unleashing powerful emotions about the way the organisation operates that they will not be able to control or contain.

Depending on where an individual sits within the organisation they will have a different perspective on this issue. Senior managers are keen to reinforce the message that racism will not be tolerated and that allegations will be treated seriously and investigated thoroughly. Middle managers subject to allegations often feel unsupported and that they must demonstrate their innocence. Staff are reluctant to make formal complaints fearing this will further damage their relationship with their manager. Human resource staff whose role is to police the organisation's policies and procedures are frequently viewed with suspicion by both sides.

It would be much healthier if senior managers made it clear that they do not view being the subject of harassment or bullying claims an indication of bad management. There can be few senior managers who have got to their current position who have not at some time been the subject of a complaint and then an investigation. Management is about setting standards, challenging poor practice and inappropriate behaviour. Management is about managing conflict, not avoiding it.

We need to recognise that protracted investigations do place both staff and managers under a lot of pressure. We recognise the need to support the complainant throughout this process but we often fail to do the same with the manager who is the subject of the complaint. The attitude is one of 'It goes with the territory'. Normally a manager would look to their line manager for support and guidance but often in these cases the line managers distance themselves on the grounds that they may need to hear the case at a later date so must remain impartial. This can sound like 'I don't want to get involved'. This is unacceptable. Line managers should be free to offer support and guidance to those they manage. This can be achieved by having a clear policy that any future hearing would be heard by a senior manager from another part of the service.

If we do not put in place proper support arrangements then some managers will not put themselves in a vulnerable or unsupported position. They will not challenge poor practice or inappropriate behaviour. This can lead to accusations by disgruntled colleagues that an individual only gets away with this because they are black – gay, disabled, a woman. Weak and inconsistent management undermines equality and diversity initiatives.

Ignoring these issues, pretending there isn't a problem, won't make them go away. We need to create a safe environment to discuss race, faith, disability, gender, age and sexuality. We need to convince staff we will treat all allegations of bullying or harassment seriously. We need to convince staff we will challenge poor performance and inappropriate behaviour whatever the race, faith, disability, gender, age or sexuality of the individual. We need to support individuals making a complaint and we need to support managers who are the subject of a complaint. There are no contradictions here: it's about treating everybody fairly.

Section 8 **Creating a Safe Place**

Small group discussion questions

1. What would a safe organisation look like?

2. To what extent could the word 'racism' be replaced by 'sexism' or 'ageism' and be equally true?

3. How damaging is it for an individual or a manager to be called racist/sexist/ageist?

4. You can't tell people what to think but you can tell them how to behave at work. What implications does this statement have for challenging racism?

5. It's all about challenging stereotypes, myths, ignorance and unthinking prejudice. To do this you need facts, information, real life examples, the opportunity to meet people who are different to you and the confidence to talk openly. Or is there more to challenging racism than this?

Further Information
www.cre.gov.uk – Commission for Race Equality
www.eoc.org.uk – Equal Opportunities Commission
www.drc-gb.org – Disability Rights Commission

Section 9
Challenging Racism by Letting People Have Their Say

A race awareness course at Lancashire County Council highlighted the extent of misunderstandings and stereotyping among staff. This section looks at how these views were challenged with the help of the Council's Intranet site.*

An unhealthy silence can take the place of open debate if staff and managers are uncomfortable about tackling race and equality issues. You cannot confront racist views, challenge stereotypes and myths or tackle ignorance if no one is prepared to talk. The fear of being accused of being a racist tends to prevent staff and managers from openly exploring the issue of race.

Our senior management team received anecdotal evidence that such an unhealthy silence existed in parts of the directorate. This was despite its clear policies, examples of good practice, targets covering recruitment and service delivery, a champions' group to promote good practice and a black workers' support group.

However, it was feedback from the black workers' support group that provided anecdotal evidence that questioned the effectiveness of our efforts. We heard about managers being reluctant to release people to attend meetings and staff made to feel uncomfortable or that they were receiving special treatment. We heard that some people were not confident that our policies would be effective because not all managers supported them. We could not be confident that managers were promoting our policies because people were reluctant to discuss issues of race.

As part of raising awareness we introduced a two-day race and equality training session for all staff. More than 300 have attended this course so far. After the first event, the trainer identified questions that staff had raised that he was either unable to answer or that he did not think it right for him to answer as someone from outside the organisation. So we produced a management response to these questions to be published on our intranet.

---

* First published in *Community Care*, 8/9/05.

As a result, Lancashire Council's Social Services Directorate is using its internal intranet to tackle hot issues by getting the real questions out in the open. These questions have arisen out of comments made by staff in racial awareness training, feedback from members of the black workers' support group and the direct experience of managers.

The questions reveal misunderstandings, stereotypes and myths about race and racism. We have been bold and faithfully reproduced these questions and provided challenging answers. The intranet and material on it is available to all staff with access to a computer – about two-thirds of our 4,700 staff. Managers can use these questions and answers to introduce discussion in team meetings, confident in the knowledge that there is an agreed management response. The result has been to give managers increased confidence in discussing issues of race and racism.

Some of these questions made uncomfortable reading for senior managers who thought that we had made more progress than this. Some questions were shocking both in their level of ignorance and their challenge to the directorate's policies, but they actually express the views of many staff and the way they think.

Publishing the questions and answers shifts the responsibility for explaining policy from front-line managers to senior managers. As the person leading on this bold approach, I felt I was taking a risk. What if this material was picked up and quoted out of context by the local press? What if the British National Party used this material to misrepresent the council's position? Would I be challenged on the answers we had provided?

This experience has taught me that you should not ignore anecdotal evidence. Instead, you should find ways of establishing whether the experience of one individual is the same as the experience of many individuals. That to get a true picture of where your organisation is in relation to race and equality you need to get people to talk openly and to capture what comes out of that discussion. And you need to do something with this information. It has shown me that many managers lack the confidence to initiate discussions with staff and adequately explain the organisation's policies when it comes to race issues.

It is important to address the issues of confidence and trust that are raised when staff experiences are different from those which senior management say they can expect. Publishing the questions and answers on the intranet site sends out a clear message about the commitment and expectations of the directorate.

Here are a selection of questions raised by staff, along with the answers, which were published on the intranet. Each question is phrased in the staff member's own words.

What about racial equality for whites?

Racial equality is about fairness for all sections of the community both black and white. We tend to focus on racial equality for minority ethnic groups because all the information we have tells us that they are not being fairly treated. We employ fewer people from minority ethnic communities than we would expect given the profile of the local community and fewer people from minority ethnic groups use our services than we would expect, given Lancashire's population.

Why do people from minority ethnic groups get special treatment like a day centre specifically for Asian elders or a choice of different meals on wheels?

Equality is not about treating everybody the same. It's about treating people fairly which involves recognising that people have different religious beliefs, values and customs. If someone's religion means they don't eat meat then it seems fair to provide them with a choice of meals that includes a vegetarian option. Most day centres operate to meet the needs of the majority group within the population so the food and the activities are not geared up to someone from the Chinese or other ethnic minority community. It seems only fair that we should develop day centres and other services where people who share the same religion, culture and background can meet together.

Isn't equality about treating everybody the same?

No. Equality is about treating everybody fairly.

Why are some jobs open to ethnic minorities only?

The sex discrimination and race equality employment legislation allows an employer to advertise to recruit someone specifically because of their gender or race providing they can demonstrate a genuine occupational qualification. An example of this would be seeking to recruit a female carer to provide personal intimate care to a disabled young Muslim woman. This would meet the criteria because it would be culturally unacceptable for the care to be provided by a male. Very few jobs advertised by social services are restricted to someone from an ethnic minority.

Why do we need a black workers' support group?

Black workers are very much in the minority within the directorate. Some people can feel very isolated being the only black person in a team, a day centre or an office. In order to help people feel less isolated we offer the opportunity for them to get together with other people in a similar situation to theirs.

Why does everybody need racial equality training when some parts of the county have little or no minority ethnic population?

The challenge of providing a culturally sensitive and appropriate service is even greater where the minority ethnic population is smallest. If staff do not routinely come across people from minority ethnic communities they are less likely to be sensitive to the issues and more likely to lack confidence in dealing appropriately with people. If there is not an established minority ethnic community in the locality then there are unlikely to be ethnic minority voluntary groups or mosques and temples that an individual can be referred to. Therefore, racial equality training is even more important for these staff.

Section 9   **Challenging Racism by Letting People Have Their Say**

Small group discussion questions

1. What are the characteristics of an effective Equality and Diversity training course?

2. How do you measure success in Equality and Diversity training?

3. Maybe we can't change the way some people think so how should we go about changing the way they behave?

Further Information
www.cre.gov.uk – Commission for Race Equality

Section 10
We are the Champions

*How do you address the inertia and lack of passion that characterises most organisations and groups set up to address equality issues?**

Championing equality can be a lonely, frustrating and thankless task.

Where do champions draw their support from? People who are prepared to give time and energy to promoting equality can come from anywhere in the organisation. Yet most organisations set up management steering groups to monitor and evaluate progress against their equality strategies and action plans. Such groups are made up of nominated representatives rather than champions. These representatives are managers and the agendas are dull reflecting a slow bureaucratic approach to change lacking passion and not inspiring anyone. Is there another way?

12 months ago we held an away day for the Directorate's Equality and Diversity Steering Group. At the away day we decided to abolish the group.

We came to this radical decision because more and more effort was being put into persuading people to attend meetings yet attendance continued to be sporadic. People were sufficiently honest at the workshop to recognise that attendance was not a reflection of commitment and that some saw the role as limited to representing their area of service and feeding back to their locality.

We decided that what was important was to identify and support people who wanted to champion equality: people at whatever level in the organisation who had a particular interest in some aspects of equality and were prepared to put in time and energy to promote equality.

The words we came up with to describe a champion included enthusiasm, commitment, passion and willingness to speak up. We asked all the representatives to confirm, by the end of the month, that they wished to be a champion. It was made quite clear to anyone who didn't wish to be a

---

* First published in *Community Care* 30/3/06 under the heading *Bring in the Champions*.

champion that this was perfectly acceptable and they would be thanked for their work to date.

As a result:

- We lost about half of the group.

- We no longer had a fully representative group.

- Some localities and some services had no champion.

The announcement that we no longer had an Equality and Diversity Steering Group but we now had an Equality and Diversity Champions Group didn't make much of a ripple within the organisation. The distinction was lost on most people. But it did make a big difference to how we felt as champions.

The champions had another one day workshop 12 months later with 15 people plus a facilitator. We spent the day reviewing the past year, re-confirming our commitment and re-defining our role as champions.

I was the chair of the Equality and Diversity Steering Group and automatically stepped in to chair the champion group. However, now I felt under great pressure to make the meeting interesting, lively and relevant because I knew people had been released from their requirement to attend. We abandoned formal agendas and didn't do the corporate consultation work on behalf of the directorate but produced some provocative material for the intranet. We became a virtual group – one that doesn't meet often but communicated frequently.

Following the previous away day, we only met three times as a champions group. One meeting was cancelled as only three other people confirmed they could attend. However, when we reviewed what had happened over the last 12 months within the directorate we felt real progress had been made in a number of areas.

Equality and Diversity had a much higher profile within the directorate and increasingly within the organisation as a whole. Two decisions in particular seemed to reflect the change within the directorate. The decision to change a two day race equality awareness training course into a mandatory two day equality and diversity course for managers with a target that all managers in the directorate would have been on the course within five months. And the decision that all interview panels in the future should be balanced in terms of gender and race.

We agreed it was difficult for us to evidence a direct link between what we as champions had been doing and saying and the progress we noted: but nevertheless we believe we have made a difference.

Much of the day was concerned with clarifying and re-defining what a champion is and what the role of the group is. We decided that a champion is someone who has a particular interest in equality and is prepared to devote time and energy to promoting equality. A champion may have a particular interest in one or all of the following: race, gender, disability, religion, age and sexuality. We confirmed champions do not have to agree on everything. We recognised the group was a safe place to express views and rehearse arguments. We acknowledged that the group existed beyond meetings and that much communication and consultation had taken place, by e-mail, and by use of the intranet. We agreed anyone could be a champion, whatever their job, and that within the group you were a champion rather than a manager. We recognised that we had failed to encourage as many people as we would have liked to join us as champions.

We made a commitment to encourage more staff to become champions and make it easier to put themselves forward. We identified two ways to do this, a statement on the intranet saying 'e-mail any one of these champions if you would like to become a champion' and encouraging people coming off equality and diversity training courses to put themselves forward by giving their names to our champion in the training section. We decided that it doesn't matter if you don't attend the meetings, you are still a champion. We agreed that the frequency of meetings and the number attending will not be a measure of success. We will hold a minimum of three meetings a year, dates agreed in advance and meetings will go ahead whether three or 33 people can attend.

We are not sure how the champions group will evolve. We could not decide whether we wanted to be a dynamic 50 or a network of 500. We will have another workshop in 12 months time and we expect to need a bigger room.

What a champion does on a day-to-day basis

- Keeps up-to-date with what's on the equality intranet site.
- Provides material to keep intranet topical. For example, newspaper articles, new Frequently Asked Questions, links to relevant websites.

- Makes colleagues aware of what's on the intranet site.

- Challenges negative stereotypes and myths around race, gender, disability, faith, sexuality and age in the staffroom, team meetings and meetings with partner agencies.

- Supports colleagues who challenge assumptions and stereotypes.

- Participates in virtual discussion with other members of the group and encourages a wider discussion in the directorate. For example, are we over-emphasising race? Should the emphasis be on awareness training around race, gender, disability, faith, sexuality and age or the principles of equality that cut across these groups?

- Identifies themselves as an equality champion (names and contact details are published on the intranet).

- Visits mosques, temples and black and minority ethnic voluntary groups in their locality with a view to fostering better understanding and future collaborations.

- Supports colleagues attending the Black Workers Support Group.

- Increases opportunities for contact between teams and members of the black and ethnic minority community through visits and placements.

- Encourages colleagues to reflect the diversity of the population we serve by the choice of pictures in reception areas and meeting rooms including positive images of disability and old age.

- Promotes and supports work experience placements within the team for students with a disability.

Profile of Equality and Diversity Champions Group

Admin/policy/communications/contracts/ICT/information services	12
Adults (learning disabilities, physical disabilities, mental health)	5
Cultural services (adult learning, student services, libraries, museums, arts, records)	14
Human resources	3
Older people	1
Total	**35**

Section 10 **We are the Champions**

Small group discussion questions

1. How would you go about moving from a steering group of nominated representatives to a network of equality champions?

2. How do you get people to recognise the common equality threads running through issues of race and gender?

3. Senior management, in their desire to demonstrate the organisation's commitment to equality, adopt policies like balanced interview panels or mentoring schemes for under represented groups. Such initiatives can be seen by front-line staff as evidence of a lack of confidence in their managers and by staff themselves as giving preferential treatment. How can such initiatives to address inequality be introduced without causing an unintended backlash?

4. Behaviour that in a male manager would be considered assertive and decisive can be seen as aggressive and domineering in a female or black manager. How do we challenge these double standard and negative labels?

Further Information
www.adss.org.uk – ADSS Inclusivity Group
www.eoc.org.uk – Equality Opportunity Commission
www.cre.gov.uk – Commision for Racial Equality
www.drc-gb.org – Disability Rights Commission

Section 11
I Hope I Die Before I Get Old

Ageism is widespread in society. It would be naïve to think it was not present in social care. Does responsibility for services to older people in need of help and support reinforce or challenge views on age – make you less ageist or more ageist? Does it matter if those responsible for services to vulnerable people use ageist language so long as they do a good job?*

Replace the word ageist with racist and read the previous sentence again.

We have every reason to assume we will live longer, healthier and enjoy a better quality of old age than our parents and grandparents. Yet rather than being a cause for celebration this increased life expectancy is seen as at best a challenge for the Welfare State and at worst as inevitable physical and mental decline leading to dependency, loss of dignity and loss of status. Planners and politicians talk of the demographic time bomb and the media promotes the message 'youth desirable, old age inevitable'.

Old age is characterised by negative stereotypes and unsupported myths. Old age equals hearing loss, mobility problems, arthritis, incontinence and memory loss. Older people are lumped together as if everybody over a certain age suddenly becomes identical in their lifestyle, circumstances, aspirations, attitudes and concerns. They are referred to as 'the elderly' and described as lonely, afraid and often the victims of crime.

A recent report identified ageism as the single biggest form of discrimination in society today. Far more prevalent than discrimination on the grounds of race, faith, gender, sexuality or disability. And if you think age discrimination only affects those with a free bus pass and a pension book, think again. Ageism in the workforce used to affect those aged 50 and older but a recent Panorama investigation found evidence of ageism against those who are 40 and over. So ageism is getting younger.

In view of the ageism all around it would be surprising if some of it did not rub off on to social workers and care assistants.

---

* First published in *Community Care* 22/6/06 under the heading *Mind Your Tongue*.

As part of raising awareness about ageism and encouraging discussion amongst senior and middle managers we designed a one question questionnaire. Working on the assumption that the language managers use is significant and that responses to the expression 'the elderly' can be used as an indication of sensitivity to and awareness of ageism we sent out an e-mail to senior and middle managers. The e-mail required managers to select the one response (out of six) that best reflected their view of the expression 'the elderly'.

The e-mail was sent to 71 managers responsible for services to people with a learning disability, people with a physical disability or sensory impairment, people with mental health problems and older people. In addition we e-mailed managers responsible for adult learning services, museums, libraries, arts and records.

Of the 71 electronic questionnaires sent out we had 64 replies (seven of these managers felt too constrained by the six options, preferring instead to provide comments).

We had three questions in mind when we sent out the electronic questionnaire:

1. Are *local authority managers* sensitive to the use of language about age?

    The high response rate and the discussion generated indicates managers are probably sensitive to the use of language. 75% of respondents had a view that indicated the debate is worthwhile i.e. they didn't choose 'It isn't worth making an issue of'.

2. Are *social services managers* **more** sensitive to the use of language about age?

    44% of adult social services managers said the term 'the elderly' is offensive or ageist and 39% of older people's service managers held the same view. This compares to 33% of overall respondents. This would possibly indicate a higher level of sensitivity in *social services managers* to the use of language about age.

3. Are *managers responsible for older people's services* **more** sensitive to the use of language about age?

    Fewer older people's managers (15%) thought that 'It wasn't worth making an issue of' compared to any other group of respondents. This seems to indicate that *managers responsible for older people's services* are more sensitive to the use of language about age.

When the findings of the survey were fed back to managers they were interpreted in different ways. Some felt that you really couldn't draw any conclusions from such diverse responses. Others felt this was evidence that people used language in different ways depending on their experience and background but we shouldn't read too much into this. There was a plea from some quarters that we create a climate in the workplace where discussion is not inhibited by people's fear of using the wrong expressions and there are those who think that too much emphasis is put on language and that actions speak louder than words.

Section 11 **I Hope I Die Before I Get Old**

Small group discussion questions

1. What would an anti-ageist organisation look like?

2. What can we learn from other cultures' attitudes to age and older people?

3. Why should we make a distinction between adults and older people who have social care and health needs?

4. The White Paper on Health and Social Care gives Social Services and local government a key role in promoting the 'Well-being' of older people – what does this mean? What are the implications for managers and social workers?

Further Information
www.agepositive.gov.uk
www.helptheaged.org.uk
www.socialexclusion.gov.uk
www.ageconcern.org.uk
www.bgop.org.uk

Section 12
Gay May be Trendy But Have Attitudes Really Changed?

Does the number of gay characters in popular television programmes reflect a change in attitude towards gay people? Are we becoming a more broad minded and tolerant society or do stereotypes, myths and prejudices about gay men and lesbian women still exist?

If you watch Emmerdale, Coronation Street or East Enders you can't have failed to notice that every soap these days seems to have to have a gay character and a lesbian relationship. Coronation Street has Hayley (not gay but a transsexual) a woman who has switched from being a man. The same seems to be true for television programmes from America: one of their most popular comedies is 'Will and Grace' about a gay man who lives with a straight woman. Is this a case of the soaps reflecting real life? Does this indicate we are a more broad-minded and tolerant society? Do our viewing habits mean that attitudes have changed or do stereotypes, myths and prejudices about gay men and lesbian women still exist?

We asked the Directorate's 35 equality and diversity champions about two work-related scenarios to check out attitudes to gay men, lesbian women and transsexuals.

Scenario 1 A gay colleague invites you to meet them in a gay pub for a drink. Do you feel:

- Totally relaxed about this?

- A little apprehensive and wonder what it is going to be like?

- That you would rather not go, as you think people might assume you are gay?

Other comments

- I would think women would be happier going to a gay bar with a gay man, than to a gay bar with a gay woman.

- I would be anxious, but would feel quite comfortable discussing this with my gay colleague.

- I have known two transsexuals, one of whom worked in my team for a while and brought an amazing array of knowledge and sensitivities to her work. Knowing what she has gone through to make the transition, I would give her every support.

- I have never been to a gay pub: I would ask for further information about the pub.

- I regularly visited gay night clubs and often held my female friends' hand in order to get past the doorman (they sometimes didn't allow heterosexuals in).

- No problem – as long as they are not making an advance!

- I think personally sexuality is a private issue.

Scenario 2 A man in your team announces that he has always felt more comfortable as a woman and from now on intends to live as one. How do you feel about this?

- I don't believe that men can become women; to me it's like taking a tablet to change your skin colour and then saying that you are black. There are years of social conditioning that go into making us who we are, and as women that is often based on our gender. In saying that, I do believe that people have a right to live in whichever way makes them most comfortable, and if this person is most comfortable being referred to as a woman, that's OK.

- I guess it again would depend on how the 'new' person behaved, or changed. I would initially feel that they would still be the same colleague, with whom I would still have the same sorts of conversations, both of a work and a personal nature. However, if the change was also associated with a significant change of 'personality' I guess I'd need to rethink things. If they became very 'girlie' – if that's an acceptable phrase in this forum – when before they weren't, as with anyone who changes lifestyle and character, I would review how to relate to them.

Some female colleagues object to this member of staff using the female toilets. What are your feelings on this?

- The easiest answer to the question about the use of toilet may be to turn the toilets into Unisex.

- The female colleagues may feel less uncomfortable if they understand that the person's 'identity' can be seen as female: they would need to be reassured that a man who cross dresses would not have the same entitlement to use the female toilets.

- I wonder whether a female using a male toilet would invoke some concerns for males in the organisation.

- I have used a gents toilet before now, when the queue for the ladies was too long.

- This has started me thinking about why toilets are either 'ladies' or 'gents' anyway. They are unisex in our homes.

In general people seem to feel more relaxed about issues of sexuality than they do about race. What was striking was the number of people who referred to friends or relatives who were gay. This difference in attitude may be a consequence of the fact that people are more likely to have contact outside of work with someone who's gay than someone who's black. However, other studies have noticed a tendency amongst health professionals to say 'there isn't an issue, we treat everybody the same', in much the same way as they used to take a colour-blind approach to race. Nowadays it would generally be recognised that equality is not about treating everybody the same. To treat everyone the same is to ignore differences arising out of race, faith, gender, disability, age and sexuality. To provide everyone with the same food would be to ignore the fact that many people are vegetarians.

Section 12 **Gay May be Trendy, But Have Attitudes Really Changed?**

Small group discussion questions

1. Why do people find it so difficult to discuss sexuality and how can the topic be raised in a safe way in your team or organisation?

2. Do the programmes referred to in the article reflect a change in attitudes or do stereotypes, myths and prejudices about gay men and lesbian women still exist?

3. How should we respond to intolerant homophobic attitudes within other cultures and ethnic minority groups? For example, homophobic attitudes in music by some rap artists have recently drawn attention to overt homophobia in sections of the African-Caribbean community.

Further Information
www.stonewall.org.uk/
www.ageconcern.org.uk – *The Whole of Me* (2006 resource pack) Age Concern

Frequently Asked Questions

Is there an over-emphasis on race in our approach to equality and diversity?

Race and racism is a high priority locally due to the disturbances in Burnley in the recent past and concern over the success of the British National Party in local council elections. In view of recent terrorist activity it's probably more appropriate to talk about race and faith. Which would involve dispelling the myths, challenging the stereotypes and dealing with ignorance around the Islamic faith. There is an emphasis on race and faith reflecting our local population profile and the local and national issues identified above. However, this should not be to the exclusion of other disadvantaged groups. The issue should not become one of competing groups around race, gender, disability, faith, sexuality and age but about challenging inequality and promoting the principles of equality across all groups.

How should we respond to sexism in the Muslim community?

Taking account of and being sensitive to cultural differences does not mean accepting sexism. Equality and diversity is as much about gender as it is about race. Creating a women-only environment for a day service or providing a female carer is being culturally sensitive: failing to consult with Muslim women as well as Muslim men is colluding with sexism.

What is institutional racism?

Institutional racism takes the form of 'processes, attitudes and behaviour which amount to discrimination through unwitting prejudice, ignorance, thoughtlessness, and racist stereotyping which disadvantage minority ethnic people' (Macpherson, 1999).

Is racism just about black people?

Racism and racial equality is not just about black people. It includes the stigmatised eastern European asylum seeker, the Iraqi woman trapped in her own home by stone throwing yobs, the gypsies and travellers who will live for 12 years less than the rest of us and the Muslims unjustly victimised because of atrocities committed by a minority of followers of their faith.

Why do we always focus on white peoples' attitudes to black people? We know African Caribbean people don't like Asians, Muslims don't get on with Hindus, there's Black on Black violence in South Africa and one tribe trying to exterminate another in places like Rwanda.

It would appear that prejudice, stereotypes, myths and ignorance exist as much between black people as between black and white people. Just as they exist between white people and white people, for example Catholics and Protestants in Northern Ireland.

We focus on attitudes between white people and black people because in this country white people are in the majority and are most often in the position of power to make decisions like who gets a job.

We all know of Asian doctors and black newsreaders so people can do well and get the top jobs if they have the right qualifications and ambition.

Just because we have some women in top jobs does not mean it is as easy for women to get these jobs as it is men. Prejudice, ignorance and stereotyping make it more difficult. It is the same for people from black and minority ethnic communities. This is the main explanation for under-representation.

Isn't the real problem poverty and disadvantage which is suffered by both black and white sections of the community?

Poverty – the lack of money to have a lifestyle the majority of us expect – arises out of unemployment, low paid work or having to live on benefits.

Black and minority ethnic groups are disproportionately represented in the unemployed and in jobs which are low paid. If you are a Muslim you are three times more likely to be unemployed. In general people don't choose not to work and they do not prefer low paid jobs. Therefore, if people from black and minority ethnic communities are over-represented in the unemployed and those in low paid jobs, it is reasonable to conclude that this is in part due to prejudice and discrimination.

An Equality and Diversity Training Course for Managers

Exploring stereotypes, examining myths, increasing awareness and challenging prejudices in relation to gender, disability, faith, sexuality, race and age.

Course organisers: LCC Social Services Training Department and Keith Burrell, Angozo Training Consultancy

Course aims

- To provide managers with the time and space to work collectively and individually at diversity trends within the work force.

- To provide a clear understanding of how personal and institutional racism and inequalities may affect the working environment.

- To provide the opportunity for managers to look at their roles and responsibilities in managing equal opportunities policies.

- To review actions and work practices necessary for meeting equality and diversity goals and objectives within the Social Services department personally and collectively.

The course objectives are to help managers:

- Reflect on their own attitudes and beliefs in order to develop ways of thinking about people and valuing differences within the communities in which they work.

- Focus clearly on their role and responsibilities for equality and diversity in relation to the recruitment and development of staff, service delivery and service development.

- Consolidate all the strands of equality and diversity i.e., race, gender, disability, faith, sexuality and age and consider how negative stereotyping, myths, ignorance and thoughtlessness may impact on each one of them.

- Increase knowledge and understanding through up-to-date and accurate information on equality legislation.

- Acquire practical skills and competencies in delivering a service to all client groups covered by the Equal Opportunities Framework legislation including those whose colour, culture, language, gender, faith, disabilities and age may be different to their own.

- Develop strategy for personal and ongoing development in the area of change management.

DAY ONE

9.15: Arrival and refreshments
9.30: Introduction/welcome/fundamentals/course objectives

Ice breaker

Exercise 1

Diversity trend

What are some of the stereotypes and myths you are aware of in regard to people of colour, people with a disability, gender, faith, sexuality, race and age?

How would you as a manager deal with these issues personally and collectively?

What might be the consequence to the department if these stereotypes are allowed to continue as it operates on a day-to-day basis?

What rate of change do you consider necessary for managing these issues?

Feedback from groups

Exercise 2

How does prejudice, discrimination, racism and power manifest itself?

How do direct and indirect discrimination along with victimisation and oppressive practices operate?

What are the issues you face when dealing with these issues?

What should you be aware of as a manager for meeting these challenges?

Exercise 3

What is a multicultural organisation?

What do you consider to be the challenges/glass ceiling limiting advancement of women, minorities and those with a disability?

Diversity maturity

It is essential if you are to manage well in today's organisations that your actions, not just your words, consistently display positive diversity values:

- How well do you understand diversity concepts?
- What aspect of your performance do you accept responsibility for improving?
- Are you able to cope with the tensions in addressing diversity?
- Are you willing to challenge the way things are done?
- How will you know that you are doing things right?

Feedback

Close

DAY TWO

9.15 a.m. Feedback

Managing political correctness in the work place

Participants will explore the use of everyday language and what is politically correct (PC) and look at a number of contemporary issues and the current debates in this area.

Faith groups

What do you know about them?

What factors do you need to consider/take into consideration when dealing with these groups as service users and in managing staff?

What guidelines would you give to your staff to help them deal with issues of faith when providing a service?

Workforce diversity profile and monitoring

Where is the directorate now?

Equality and diversity legislation

This is intended to give participants a thorough knowledge of the equality and diversity legislations, what the legislation says and the role and responsibility of all employees of the council.

Case study

Case study and discussion

Managing diversity

Building a directorate culture that allows all individuals to meet their full potential.

Tackling diversity in the work place

Evaluate the work practices of your team and whether it is actively taking steps to bring about equality and diversity anti-discriminatory practice.

What are the issues for you as a manager?

Common areas that should be addressed:

- work environment
- caseload
- team ethos
- reports
- gate-keeping
- staffing

Bringing it all together

How to become a competent equal opportunities practitioner

Feedback

Close